Woodrow Wilson

*The warm true-life story of the
President who went to war
to save democracy*

DRAMATIZED IN
ALL-PICTORIAL PRESENTATION

Davco Publishers
SKOKIE, ILLINOIS 60076

CONSULTANTS

SARA THROOP, PH.D.
  Youngstown State University
  Youngstown, Ohio

JOAN DUFF KISE, PH.D.
  Elementary Education Department
  Kent State University
  Kent, Ohio

IDA S. MELTZER, B.A.
  Supervisor Language Arts
  Marine Park Junior High School
  Brooklyn, New York

SYLVIA E. DAVIS, M.S.A.E.
  Chairman Art Department
  Waller High School
  Chicago, Illinois

MORRIS R. BUSKE, M.A.
  Instructor Social Studies
    Department
  Triton College
  River Grove, Illinois

DOROTHY L. GROSS, B.S.M.S.
  Instructor Art Department
  Detroit Public Schools
  Detroit, Michigan

EDITORIAL AND ART

Executive Editor
  JANET TEGLAND, M.A.
  Coordinator Learning
    Disabilities Department
  Top of the World School
  Laguna Beach Unified School
    District
  Laguna Beach, California
  Instructor Creative Writing
  Saddleback Community College
  Mission Viejo, California

Artists
  TOM JOHNSON
  MELVIN KEEFER
  CARLOS NORTE
  ROBERT GOLDIN
  JANICE SALTZ

Historical Researchers
  THOMAS MCLAUGHLIN
  BARBARA MCCORMICK
  BERTHA RABENS

Art and Editorial Production
  HOWARD PARKS
  CARYL KURTZMAN
  ARLINE BLOCK
  GAIL GOLDBERG
  JOSEPH POSTILION
  NICK CURCIO
  HERBERT BUCHHOLZ
  RONALD FALK

© MCMLXXVI Davco Publishers
Skokie, Illinois 60076

Library of Congress catalog card No. 75-12244
ISBN No. 0-89233-005-8

Only governments and not people initiate wars. . . . Democracy, therefore, is the best preventive of such jealousies and suspicions and secret intrigues as produce wars among nations where small groups control rather than the great body of public opinion.

WOODROW WILSON
November, 1916

Table of Contents

In 1916, Woodrow Wilson was elected to a second term as President of the United States. The nations of Europe were at war.

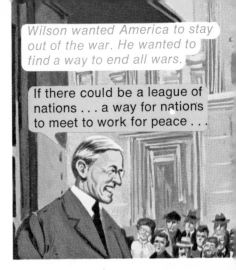

Wilson wanted America to stay out of the war. He wanted to find a way to end all wars.

If there could be a league of nations . . . a way for nations to meet to work for peace . . .

But he was not willing to accept peace at any cost.

We have received word that Germany is going to wage submarine warfare on all ships.

In March, 1917, Germany started sinking American ships.

On April 2, 1917, Wilson called a special session of Congress . . . and America entered World War I.

The world must be made safe for democracy.

The man who was to lead America in World War I was born on December 28, 1856, in Staunton, Virginia.

Congratulations, Reverend. With two daughters, I know you were hoping for a son.

While Woodrow was still a baby, his family moved to Augusta, Georgia.

We'll miss you, Reverend. Good luck at your new church.

Woodrow was too young in 1860 to understand the problems that were leading to a civil war between Northern and Southern states.

Lincoln has been elected President.

Then there will be war.

His father tried to help his son understand the world he was growing up in.

When men believe they have to settle their problems by fighting, that makes a war, son.

What makes a war, Father?

The horrors of the Civil War made a lasting impression on Woodrow. He came to hate war. His father's church was used as a hospital for wounded soldiers in the Confederate army.

It was awful. The Yankees kept coming and coming and coming.

Sssh. Rest now.

The land behind the church was used as a prison for Northern soldiers

Food was hard to find during the war.

Cowpea soup.

Ugh! What's this?

We *used* to feed cowpeas to our cattle.

Our service will be short. I want you all to go to the gunpowder factory and help make bullets.

But no matter how bad the war was, the Wilson family gathered together each night to sing, talk, and to read the Bible.

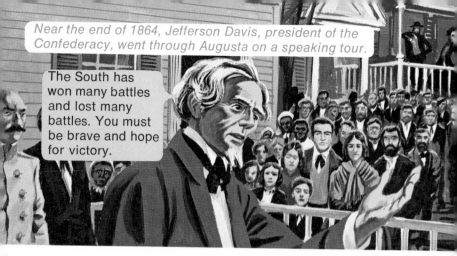

Near the end of 1864, Jefferson Davis, president of the Confederacy, went through Augusta on a speaking tour.

The South has won many battles and lost many battles. You must be brave and hope for victory.

A few months later, President Davis passed through Augusta again—as a prisoner of war.

The South has lost.

The government is setting up a Freedmen's Bureau. They will have schools, and learn how to take care of themselves.

What will happen to the slaves?

After the war, 5,000 slaves were set free in Augusta. But they did not have any food or homes.

Because of the war, young Woodrow had never gone to school. His father had taught him how to read and write. When he was nine, he was sent to a school run by Joseph Derry, an ex-Confederate army officer.

He did not like school.

You do not know your Latin, Master Wilson.

I'll never learn it.

When a circus came through Augusta, Woodrow and his friends skipped school.

And . . . they had to accept their punishment.

In 1870, when Woodrow was fourteen, his father was named professor at the Presbyterian seminary in Columbia, South Carolina. Columbia had been badly damaged during the war.

General Sherman's army burned this city. It will take a long time to rebuild it.

Woodrow started to show his ability as a student when he attended a school run by Charles Barnwell.

You're good with the younger boys. I'd like you to help them with their lessons.

But Woodrow learned more from his father than from any teacher.

Make your mind like a needle— one eye and a single point. Shoot your words straight at the target.

His father gave him a key to the seminary library —and Woodrow read everything.

In 1873, Woodrow went to Davidson College near Charlottesville, North Carolina. It was his first time away from his family.

He studied hard, because he was behind the other students in his school work.

He loved sports at college, especially baseball.

He joined the debating society and became an outstanding public speaker.

Our subject today is the death of Lincoln.

He worked so hard that he was ill when he went home in June.

You look terrible.

His family moved again that fall—to a seaport town in North Carolina. Woodrow was not well enough to go back to Davidson College.

You must exercise and eat good food.

His father gave him a bicycle, and he spent many hours at the harbor.

But he spent most of his time inside, reading adventure stories.

You spend too much time alone. Come with me to the church social.

You'll soon be well enough to go back to school. I want you to go to Princeton in September.

Princeton was 500 miles away. It was the first time Woodrow had ever been in the North. At first, he was lonely . . .

. . . but as soon as he joined the debating society, he had many friends.

I want to be able to convince people, without using anger.

He found that few Northern students understood how people in the South felt.

Slavery was evil. The South was evil.

You couldn't speak like that if you knew anything about the South.

He also found there were things he didn't know.

What is that song?

The Star-Spangled Banner.

At Princeton, he became deeply interested in politics. He hated the way Republican President Grant had treated the South after the war, and hoped the Democrats would win in 1876.

I know you wanted me to be a minister, Father. But I think I want to be in government.

He became known at Princeton as an outstanding speaker . . .

Wilson is debating tonight. He's always good.

DEBATE TONIGHT

W. WILSON
M. BRANCH

UNITED STATE
GOVERNMENT
ISSUES AND
ANSWERS

. . . and as a good writer.

Cabinet Government of the United States by Woodrow Wilson

With the money he earned from the sale of his first article, he bought a bookcase.

I want that one.

14

After graduating from Princeton, he enrolled in law school at the University of Virginia.

Law is dull. It's like having hash for dinner every night.

He continued his writing and public speaking . . .

JEFFERSON SOCIETY DEBATE THOMAS WOODROW WILSON AND WILLIAM CABELL BRUCE

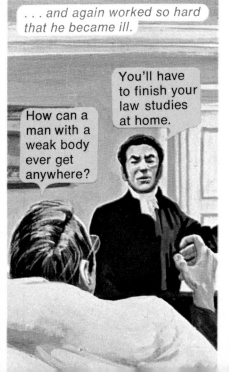

. . . and again worked so hard that he became ill.

You'll have to finish your law studies at home.

How can a man with a weak body ever get anywhere?

In June, 1882, he received his law degree.

Now I must begin to earn my own living.

Wilson went to Atlanta, Georgia, and joined his friend Edward Renick in setting up a law firm. But there were too many lawyers in Atlanta already.

Nobody has come through that door in a week.

Walter Hines Page, a reporter for the New York World newspaper, came to visit Renick.

The U.S. Tariff Commission is holding a hearing on tariff laws. I'm writing the story for my paper.

What're you doing in Atlanta, Walter?

Wilson believed that the tariff—a tax on goods brought in from other countries—was too high.

America cannot trade with other countries in the world as long as we have a high tariff. Other countries don't like it.

Why don't you talk to the commission?

Wilson did. It was his first real public debate.

American businessmen *must* compete with the rest of the world.

His speech was a great success. And he knew that he had to find a way to explain his ideas on how governments should be run.

I don't think being a lawyer is what I want.

Johns Hopkins University is offering a new subject— political science.

While Wilson was thinking about going to Johns Hopkins, he was finally hired as a lawyer.

Who hired you as a lawyer?

My mother.

Wilson went to Rome, Georgia to handle some legal work for his mother. While attending church, he met the minister's daughter.

And this is my daughter, Ellen.

I hear your father is a minister, too.

The two were soon in love.

I won't go to Johns Hopkins. I'll get a job so we can marry right away.

No. We can wait. Find what it is you want to do with your life.

17

Wilson went to Johns Hopkins in Baltimore. Meanwhile, Ellen studied painting. They wrote each other often.

Wilson decided to write a book describing how the government functions under a weak President.

Did you finish the chapter, Woodrow?

When he finished his book, he titled it Congressional Government. A publisher bought it quickly.

They are paying me as much as a well-known writer. Wait until I tell Ellen!

Wilson graduated from Johns Hopkins in June, 1885—and he and Ellen were married a few weeks later.

18

Wilson accepted an offer to teach history at Bryn Mawr College in Pennsylvania.

Bryn Mawr? I've never heard of it.

It's a new Quaker college for women.

He was often shy before his all-girl classes.

To cover up his shyness, he made himself seem very cross—and then worried about it.

I told a joke in class today, and no one laughed. They all wrote it down. How dull I must seem.

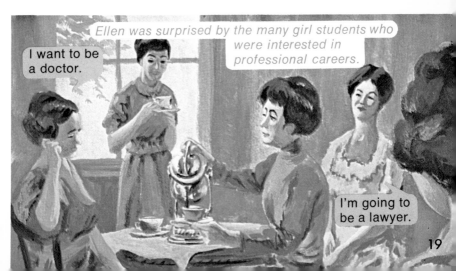

Ellen was surprised by the many girl students who were interested in professional careers.

I want to be a doctor.

I'm going to be a lawyer.

Wilson taught at Bryn Mawr for two years, but then began to grow restless.

Oh, Woodrow! You're a good teacher. Your second book is about to be published.

I am thirty-one. I have done nothing with my life.

When he was asked to teach at Wesleyan University in Connecticut, he quickly said yes.

The salary is higher, and I'll feel better teaching men.

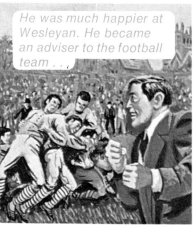

He was much happier at Wesleyan. He became an adviser to the football team . . .

. . . organized a debating society . . .

Make your mind like a needle . . .

. . . and helped the college set up a new "electives" program.

The students should be allowed to choose some of the courses they want to take.

His second year at Wesleyan was filled with excitement. His new book was published, and critics liked it.

NOW ON SALE
THE STATE
BY
WOODROW WILSON

His third daughter was born in October, 1889.

Let's name her Eleanor.

He was so popular as a public speaker, he was often asked to speak at other universities.

In 1890, Princeton offered him a job teaching law and political history.

Ellen! Ellen! We're moving to New Jersey!

Wilson knew he wanted to stay at Princeton for a long time, there was so much to do.

Students cheat on tests, and nobody does anything. And entrance exams are so easy, anybody can get into Princeton.

He made his own courses hard, and students who did not work did not pass.

Wilson is a hard teacher, but he's good.

I know. He makes history seem so real.

He enjoyed riding his bicycle around the Princeton campus.

His third book, Division and Reunion, was published in 1893.

What is your new book about?

How America healed its wounds after the Civil War.

When the students wanted to be placed on the honor system, Wilson agreed with them, even though the president of Princeton was opposed.

Students *must* be watched during tests.

They should be given the chance to be on their honor.

After that, the students knew he was on their side.

Hurrah for Professor Wilson!

Wilson was asked to write a history of the American people.

I've always dreamed of writing such a book.

But no matter how busy he was, he found time in the evening to spend with his family.

Wilson was working too hard, and Ellen knew it. In 1896, his right hand became crippled.

He needs to get more rest.

Ellen said that he should go to the British Isles for a rest.

He visited the towns in Scotland where his great-grandfather had been a minister.

He visited Oxford University, and last of all, London.

When he returned home, he was well rested and eager to get back to teaching.

My arm hardly hurts at all.

When Wilson came back to America in 1896, the Democrats had named William Jennings Bryan to run for President against Republican William McKinley. Wilson was worried about the Democratic party under Bryan.

He's a great speaker. But I don't like his ideas on government.

But Wilson had the problems of Princeton to worry about, and an important speech to write.

Princeton will be 150 years old in October. I am to make one of the main speeches.

He spent many hours writing the speech. He knew important people would be listening.

I have dreamed about a perfect place of learning . . .

Wilson had plans for improving Princeton and the country. But he was saddened when America went to war with Spain in 1898.

Although disappointed by America's declaring war on Spain, he was pleased when the United States helped set up a world peace court.

Wilson was so upset at the president of Princeton for blocking his plans for improvement, he offered to resign.

I'm tired. I think I would like to spend all my time writing.

And then he received news that changed his plans.

The president of Princeton has quit. We want you to be the new president.

Wilson began to make his dreams for Princeton come true. He made the classes harder so that only students who wanted to work and to learn could remain in school.

I know you are a good football player. But you must also study history if you want to stay at Princeton.

He started a "preceptor" system, and insisted that students study many subjects but specialize in one.

Preceptors are like assistant professors. They will help the students, and they will help the professors.

Now every student at Princeton can have help when he needs it.

At the end of Wilson's first year as president, his father died.

He taught me more than anyone.

27

When Republican Theodore Roosevelt was elected President of the U.S. on his own in 1904, Wilson watched to see if the President would push the reforms he promised.

America must speak softly but carry a big stick.

Wilson still worried about William Jennings Bryan as leader of the Democratic party.

I'm afraid many of Bryan's ideas are unworkable in the U.S.

At a dinner given to honor Wilson, one of the speakers made a surprising prediction.

I believe the president of Princeton could be a great President of the United States.

Was he joking?

He didn't seem to be.

2

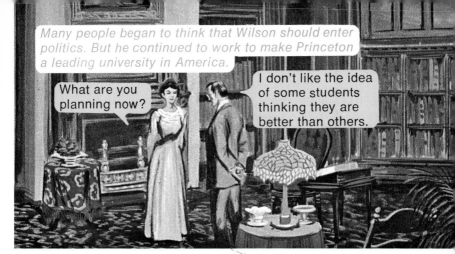

Many people began to think that Wilson should enter politics. But he continued to work to make Princeton a leading university in America.

What are you planning now?

I don't like the idea of some students thinking they are better than others.

Wilson presented a new plan to the university's trustees.

I don't want any more special clubs at Princeton. I want all students to be equal —live together, study together—in specially built quads.

The trustees did not like Wilson's plan.

Wilson's plan would cost money. It would be better to spend that money on the graduate school.

In 1907, Wilson was told to withdraw his plan.

29

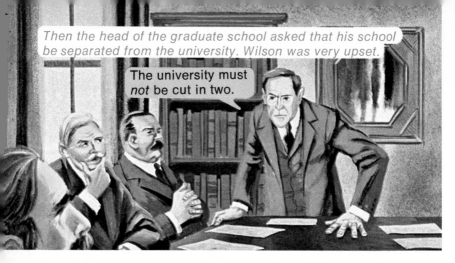

Then the head of the graduate school asked that his school be separated from the university. Wilson was very upset.

The university must *not* be cut in two.

But the graduate school dean had many rich men behind him.

I'll give half a million dollars if your plan is passed.

Wilson was angry and attacked rich men's control of colleges.

A danger surrounding our modern education is the danger of wealth. Money can be dangerous to education.

People began to listen to him and to think of him as a leader.

We'd like you to write a story for the *New York Times*.

Wilson knew there were many things wrong with government in New Jersey.

Gambling should not be allowed. Big companies shouldn't get special tax treatment.

The people loved to hear him speak, but many made fun of his looks.

You're all right, Woody. But you ain't no beaut.

I must remember that.

When election day came, the Wilsons waited for the results in their home.

Too bad women can't vote. You'd have four more votes.

At ten o'clock that night, Wilson heard the news.

We won!

Soon after the election, Wilson was asked to prove he wouldn't give favors to anyone. James Smith, Jr., the Democratic leader, wanted to be named U.S. senator.

I believe the people want another man.

I will be senator.

Wilson let the people decide. He told them about the problem.

Your letters to me, and to your legislators, will decide who your senator will be.

The people did not choose Smith.

Wilson has everything his way now. But our turn will come.

Wilson made many changes including direct election primaries and workmen's compensation. But Smith blocked other reforms.

My bill didn't pass today.

A New York state senator, Franklin Delano Roosevelt, came to see Wilson.

I would like to see you run for President. I think New York will vote for you.

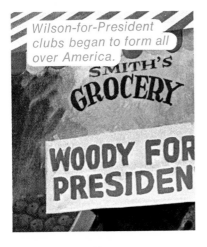

Wilson-for-President clubs began to form all over America.

SMITH'S GROCERY

WOODY FOR PRESIDEN

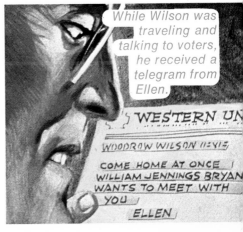

While Wilson was traveling and talking to voters, he received a telegram from Ellen.

WESTERN UN

WOODROW WILSON 11=415

COME HOME AT ONCE WILLIAM JENNINGS BRYAN WANTS TO MEET WITH YOU

ELLEN

Wilson had not liked Bryan's ideas—but he liked the man.

You have my support, Woodrow, for the Democratic party's nomination for President.

Wilson traveled across America, telling the people what he believed in.

More than any other thing, I want world peace.

I want taxes on goods from other countries lowered.

He was invited to speak before many groups.

I'm sorry. I don't make speeches on Sunday. I go to church.

But we want you to talk about the Bible.

Any man who knows the Bible that well must read it every day.

Smith and others who disliked Wilson tried to stop him. The New York Sun newspaper printed a letter Wilson had written five years earlier.

EDITOR IN CHIEF

Wilson said he'd like to see William Jennings Bryan knocked into a cocked hat.

He shouldn't say that. Bryan's a good man.

At a dinner a few days later, Bryan had his picture taken with his arm around Wilson.

They won't stop us that easily, Woodrow.

Wilson waited at his seashore home for the results of the Democratic convention.

CLARK 440½
WILSON 324
HARMON 148
UNDERWOOD 117½

On the first ballot, Wilson ran second.

After more than forty ballots, Wilson finally was declared the winner.

Wilson had to convince many people that he would make a good President. Some blacks were uneasy about electing a President who was born in the South.

I want what is best for all people.

Women's groups knew he was against women voting.

WILSON NO

He convinced the workingman that he wanted to help him.

You know I was against rich men running Princeton.

Worried about his crippled hand, he held his fingers very loosely when shaking hands with voters.

What a cold handshake!

Wilson was running against the Republican party candidate, President William Howard Taft, and the Progressive party candidate, Teddy Roosevelt. Wilson and Roosevelt spoke out for reform of big business. But they seldom agreed on how to make changes.

You need a bodyguard.

Teddy Roosevelt has been shot while campaigning!

His advisers sent for a six-foot-tall former Texas Ranger.

I don't want a bodyguard.

This man can hit the eye of a mosquito from 50 yards away. And you need him.

Wilson ended his campaign in New York City.

We want Wilson, we want Wilson!

A message came to Ellen at 10 p.m. on election night.

You are the new President of the United States.

Soon after Wilson became President, the U.S. became involved in the revolution that broke out in Mexico. The president of Mexico was killed by one of his generals, Huerta.

Many Americans wanted Wilson to accept Huerta as the new leader of Mexico.

But what about the Mexican people? Is this what they want?

He sent a special agent to Mexico.

Tell Huerta America will accept him if he gives the people of Mexico an election, and they elect him.

Huerta would not agree with Wilson's demands.

Tell your President I said no.

While Wilson was worrying about Mexico, many changes were taking place in his family. His oldest daughter, Jessie, was married in the White House.

This is the first break in our family.

Their youngest daughter planned to marry in May.

I want to marry William.

Ellen's health began to fail.

I'm sorry, Woodrow. Ellen is very sick.

Wilson took his wife to West Virginia for a rest—but was called back to Washington by an urgent message from the secretary of state.

Yes, of course. I'll come right away.

American navy officers were being arrested by Huerta in Mexico.

Wilson went to Congress.

I want to use our armed forces in Mexico if needed.

While Congress was deciding what to do, a German ship arrived in the Mexican town of Vera Cruz with arms for the Mexicans.

Send this message to Admiral Fletcher: Attack the port of Vera Cruz.

Several American lives were lost, but the port was captured.

Three South American countries asked Wilson to let them help settle the Mexican trouble. A conference was held in Canada.

The Mexican people will elect their own leader.

And America will withdraw her troops.

As soon as the trouble with Mexico was over, there was new trouble in Europe.

Germany is getting ready to make war on all of Europe.

On August 1, 1914, Germany declared war on Russia.

Wilson sent a message to the nations of Europe.

"The United States wishes to help you settle your problems without war."

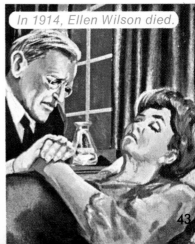

In 1914, Ellen Wilson died.

43

Wilson missed Ellen very much.

This is the loneliest place in the world.

But America's problems and the world's problems left little time for sadness.

The war has made it clearer than ever . . . nations must learn to work together for peace.

Wilson believed America could bring about world peace by staying out of the war.

America must not take sides.

Many agreed—but some did not.

America cannot stay out of this war. This is a *world* war.

The war in Europe was of vital concern to Wilson. The Germans started using a new kind of weapon—the submarine. German subs sailed near England, and threatened to sink any ship coming close.

Wilson's doctor was very concerned about his health.

Woodrow, you must stop working so hard.

Oh, be quiet! Do you know who that woman is?

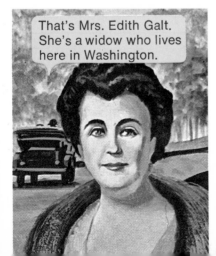

That's Mrs. Edith Galt. She's a widow who lives here in Washington.

On May 7, 1915, the Germans torpedoed the British ship Lusitania. 124 Americans on board died when the ship sank.

Wilson wrote Germany that any more submarine attacks harming American citizens would lead to war. He met with the secretary of the navy and the secretary of war.

I want you to plan a program for a bigger army and navy.

Secretary of State Bryan resigned.

I believe your protests have been too strong for a neutral.

I'm trying as hard as I can to keep peace.

Wilson's doctor made sure that Woodrow met Edith Galt.

Have you ever thought of marrying again, Edith?

Since meeting you, I have.

Wilson and Edith became engaged. Wilson's enemies began to gossip.

They say he knew Mrs. Galt before his wife died.

His wife has been dead only a year.

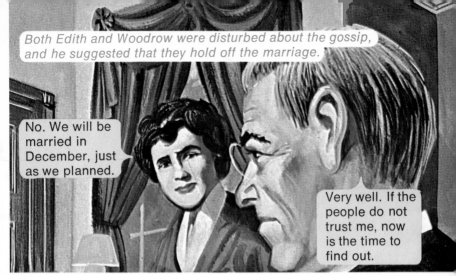

Both Edith and Woodrow were disturbed about the gossip, and he suggested that they hold off the marriage.

No. We will be married in December, just as we planned.

Very well. If the people do not trust me, now is the time to find out.

They were married in December, 1915, in Edith's home.

Still hoping America could lead the world powers to end the war, Wilson sent his close friend, Colonel House, to Europe.

Tell them again that America wants to help them make peace.

But he knew America might not be able to stay out of the war.

We're going to travel across America, and tell the people why we must have a stronger army.

There is a price too great to pay for peace . . . self-respect.

47

Colonel House returned to the United States . . . with bad news.

We will have to go to war with Germany. It will not stop destroying unarmed ships.

I'm going to try once more to make Germany listen to reason.

In May, Germany signed the "Sussex Pledge," promising not to attack any more unarmed ships.

Wilson gave a speech at a meeting of the League to Enforce Peace.

I propose to you a plan for a league of nations . . .

Wilson ran again for President in 1916 against Republican Charles Evans Hughes. The election was close. Wilson did not know for three days if he had won or lost. He won by only 500,000 votes.

WILSON HE KEPT US OUT OF WAR!

WE WANT WILSON

ILLINOIS

VIRGINIA

4

Germany broke its Sussex Pledge, and the U.S. Congress declared war. Wilson worked as hard to win the war as he had to make peace. The U.S. military insisted that young men register for the draft.

Isn't this the day you are supposed to register for the draft?

Wilson did not like the idea of drafting soldiers, but he was forced to go along with the military.

Since taxes alone could not pay for the war, the government sold Liberty Bonds.

Americans are buying $20 million worth of bonds every hour.

Millions of Americans tried to save food by growing their own vegetables.

At the time America declared war, the Germans held a long line of defense that French and British troops could not break. Training camps were established in many areas of the U.S. to teach the new soldiers how to handle guns.

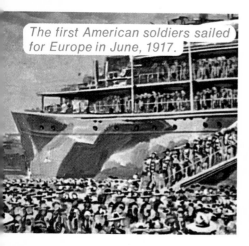

The first American soldiers sailed for Europe in June, 1917.

Thank God. Not one ship was torpedoed.

Near the end of 1917, the Communists overthrew the Russian government and made peace with Germany.

Russia will no longer help us fight the Germans.

That means Germany will not have to fight in the East. It can send thousands more soldiers against the West.

Wilson acted fast.

Our soldiers must be moved faster. I'm placing railroads under government control.

He ordered Americans to have "heatless days" to save coal.

When a labor union wanted to stop work, Wilson sent them an angry message.

Will you help the war effort, or will you hurt it?

England, France, and Italy could not agree on how to end the war. Wilson spent long hours explaining his "Fourteen Points for Peace."

There must be freedom of the sea in peace and war . . .

The Germans sent thousands of soldiers to fight in the West in May, 1918. American troops arrived in France in late July, and helped drive the Germans back.

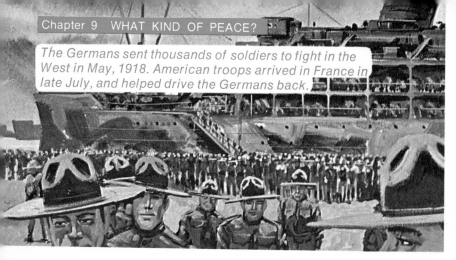

The Germans began to believe they might lose the war.

Tell Wilson we are ready to discuss his fourteen-point peace plan.

Their submarines are still sinking ships. They are not really ready for peace.

Bitter at the prospect of losing the war, the German people rose up against their government.

Since France, England, and Italy were not ready to make peace with Germany, Wilson threatened the countries who fought alongside the Americans.

Then America will make peace alone with Germany.

Many did not agree with Wilson. And it was time for the American people to elect new senators and representatives.

Wilson is wrong. There should be no 'peace without victory.'

We should destroy Germany's cities.

Wilson asked the people for their help.

If you have approved of me . . . return Democrats to the House and Senate.

But Republicans were elected, and Wilson lost control of the House of Representatives and the Senate.

I'm going to plan for peace anyway. Some of them will support me.

On November 11, 1918, Germany and America, France, and England agreed to stop fighting.

"My fellow countrymen . . . Everything for which America fought has been accomplished . . ."

Wilson began at once to bring about his dream— a league of nations.

We will hold a conference in Paris to work out a peace treaty.

Wilson decided to go to the conference himself.

The President should stay at home.

Too many countries will want favors. The President should stay out of it.

But Wilson insisted on attending. He sailed on December 4, 1918.

A long red carpet was spread out at the railroad station in Paris for the Wilsons.

On January 18, 1919, the conference opened.

Four men were chosen as leaders.

GEORGES CLEMENCEAU FRANCE

DAVID LLOYD GEORGE ENGLAND

WOODROW WILSON AMERICA

VITTORIO ORLANDO ITALY

Wilson's doctor warned him that he was working too hard.

Slow down, Woodrow.

I can't. The world needs a lasting peace after this terrible war.

Wilson asked that a league of nations be formed to keep world peace. The Covenant of the League of Nations was approved as part of the peace treaty.

The President had to return to America for the last session of Congress.

I feel I have kept faith with the people.

Wilson gave copies of the Covenant to members of the House and Senate.

Work hard for it. It could mean an end to all war.

He returned to the Peace Conference in Paris in June, 1919 to sign the Versailles Treaty.

It is not all I hoped for. But it is a beginning.

When Wilson returned to America, he found that his political enemies opposed the League of Nations. He decided that once again he would have to travel and talk directly to the people.

If you go on such a tour, it could kill you.

If the League fails, I hate to think what will happen to the world.

His special train left Washington in September, 1919.

This treaty is the first of its kind in history.

For three weeks, he spoke in halls, in tents, and from the back of his train.

Speaking many times a day made Wilson very tired. In Colorado, he collapsed, and the rest of the tour had to be cancelled.

Get the President home at once.

57

At home in Washington, Wilson's health did not improve. He was awarded the Nobel Peace Prize in 1919, and suffered a stroke the same year.

In March, 1920, the Senate voted against the U.S. joining a world league of nations. Wilson was shocked.

They cannot know what they have done.

The 1920 Democratic candidate for President, James Cox, and his running mate, Franklin Roosevelt, promised Wilson they would support the treaty if elected.

Mr. President, we are a million per cent with you.

But Republican Warren G. Harding was elected President, and the United States never joined the League of Nations.

Woodrow Wilson died on February 3, 1924. His dream for a world peace organization did not come true until twenty-one years later, when the United Nations was created during the final months of World War II.

Significant Places in the Life of Woodrow Wilson

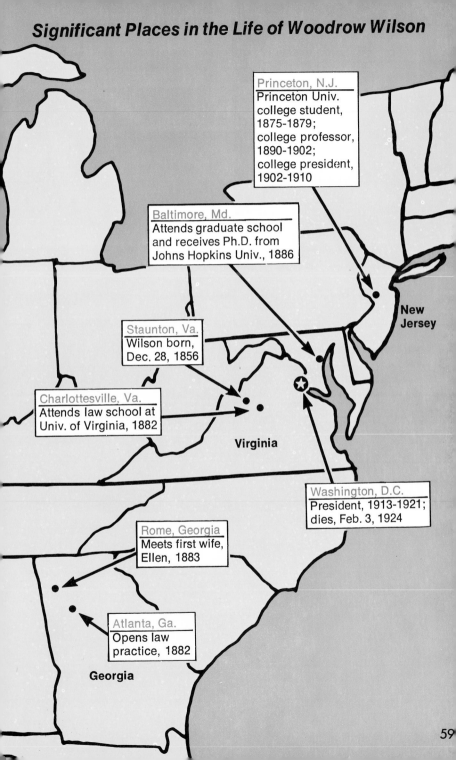

Princeton, N.J.
Princeton Univ.
college student,
1875-1879;
college professor,
1890-1902;
college president,
1902-1910

Baltimore, Md.
Attends graduate school
and receives Ph.D. from
Johns Hopkins Univ., 1886

Staunton, Va.
Wilson born,
Dec. 28, 1856

Charlottesville, Va.
Attends law school at
Univ. of Virginia, 1882

Washington, D.C.
President, 1913-1921;
dies, Feb. 3, 1924

Rome, Georgia
Meets first wife,
Ellen, 1883

Atlanta, Ga.
Opens law
practice, 1882

New Jersey

Virginia

Georgia

Historical Events During th•

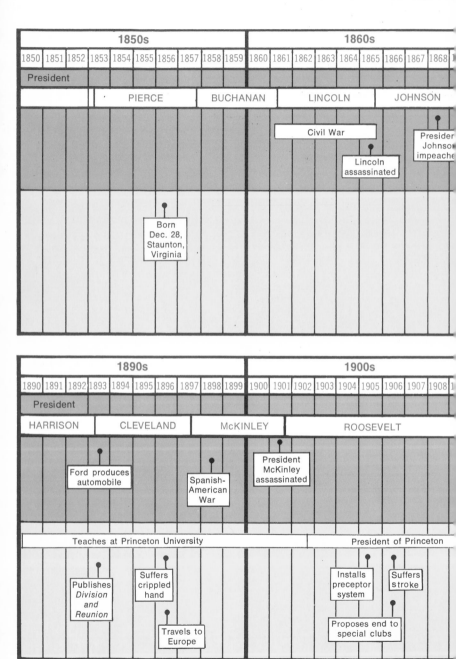

1850s										1860s									
1850	1851	1852	1853	1854	1855	1856	1857	1858	1859	1860	1861	1862	1863	1864	1865	1866	1867	1868	

President

PIERCE — BUCHANAN — LINCOLN — JOHNSON

Civil War

Lincoln assassinated

Presider
Johnson
impeache

Born
Dec. 28,
Staunton,
Virginia

1890s										1900s									
1890	1891	1892	1893	1894	1895	1896	1897	1898	1899	1900	1901	1902	1903	1904	1905	1906	1907	1908	

President

HARRISON — CLEVELAND — McKINLEY — ROOSEVELT

Ford produces automobile

Spanish-American War

President McKinley assassinated

Teaches at Princeton University — President of Princeton

Publishes *Division and Reunion*

Suffers crippled hand

Travels to Europe

Installs preceptor system

Proposes end to special clubs

Suffers stroke

60

Lifetime of Woodrow Wilson

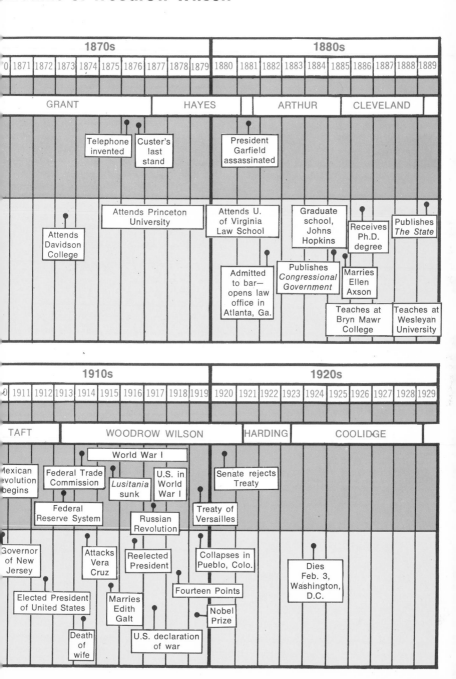

1870s

'0 | 1871 | 1872 | 1873 | 1874 | 1875 | 1876 | 1877 | 1878 | 1879

1880s

1880 | 1881 | 1882 | 1883 | 1884 | 1885 | 1886 | 1887 | 1888 | 1889

GRANT — HAYES — ARTHUR — CLEVELAND

Telephone invented
Custer's last stand
President Garfield assassinated

Attends Princeton University
Attends Davidson College
Attends U. of Virginia Law School
Graduate school, Johns Hopkins
Receives Ph.D. degree
Publishes *The State*
Admitted to bar— opens law office in Atlanta, Ga.
Publishes *Congressional Government*
Marries Ellen Axson
Teaches at Bryn Mawr College
Teaches at Wesleyan University

1910s

0 | 1911 | 1912 | 1913 | 1914 | 1915 | 1916 | 1917 | 1918 | 1919

1920s

1920 | 1921 | 1922 | 1923 | 1924 | 1925 | 1926 | 1927 | 1928 | 1929

TAFT — WOODROW WILSON — HARDING — COOLIDGE

World War I
Mexican Revolution begins
Federal Trade Commission
Lusitania sunk
U.S. in World War I
Senate rejects Treaty
Federal Reserve System
Russian Revolution
Treaty of Versailles
Governor of New Jersey
Attacks Vera Cruz
Reelected President
Collapses in Pueblo, Colo.
Dies Feb. 3, Washington, D.C.
Elected President of United States
Fourteen Points
Marries Edith Galt
Nobel Prize
Death of wife
U.S. declaration of war

GLOSSARY

The meanings and pronunciations of words found in this book.

advisers *(ăd-vī'zərz)*
people close to a President who offer advice and information

agent *(ā'jənt)*
a messenger; one who is given the power or right to speak or act on behalf of another, or a government

assistant *(ə-sĭs'tənt)*
a helper; an aide

ballot *(băl'ət)*
a system of voting; votes are taken on each *ballot* until there is a majority winner. You also vote in an election by marking a *ballot* with your choice.

bill *(bĭl)*
a plan for a law. You can also pay a *bill;* or spend a dollar *bill.* A bird's beak is called a *bill.*

bodyguard *(bŏd'ē-gärd)*
a person who is hired to protect another from harm

break *(brāk)*
to reduce by separation; Jessie broke the family unit by marrying and leaving home. If you *break* a link, the chain will fall apart.

campaign *(kăm-pān')*
a series of operations designed or planned to help obtain a goal—such as to elect a candidate or reduce air and water pollution

commission *(kə-mĭsh'ən)*
a group of people given the job of studying a subject

conference *(kŏn'fə-rəns)*
a meeting for discussion or consultation on plans or ideas; you can have a *conference* with an adviser on your school work. Your mother usually attends a Parents-Teachers *Conference.*

Congress *(kŏng'grĭs)*
the elected representatives from all states in the U.S.

covenant *(kŭv'ə-nənt)*
an agreement between parties—in this case between nations

cowpea *(kōu'pē)*
a vine with long, hanging pods grown in the southern U.S.; used as animal feed

degree *(dĭ-grē')*
an academic title given by a college or university to a student who successfully completes a course of study

democracy *(dĭ-mŏk'rə-sē)*
government by the people either directly or through elected representatives

draft
the system under which adult males had to register for military service, and were chosen through a lottery drawing to report for duty

electives *(ĭ-lĕk'tĭvs)*
classes or studies students choose to take; not required courses

favors *(fā'vərz)*
advantages given after election in return for political support

Freedmen's Bureau
(frēd'mĕns byoor'ō)
a government office set up after the Civil War to protect the rights of newly freed slaves and help them adjust to a new life

hara-kiri *(hăr'ə-kîr'ē)*
ritual suicide by disembowelment, formerly practiced by the Japanese upper class

harbor *(här'bər)*
a sheltered part of a body of water deep enough to provide anchorage for ships

honor system *(ŏn'ər sĭs'təm)*
with this system, students take tests without close supervision; they are on their honor not to cheat.

labor union *(lā'bər yoōn'yən)*
a group formed for a common purpose; usually to protect the rights of, and give benefits to, the workingman

law school
a college specializing in legal studies (rules used to govern) leading to a degree in law.

league *(lēg)*
an organization—meeting of people—come together for a common purpose or action; you know about the National Football League.

GLOSSARY

legislators *(lĕj´ĭs-lā-tərs)*
members of a government body
that creates or enacts laws

Liberty Bonds
(lĭb´ər-tē bŏnds)
bonds or certificates offered for
sale by the U.S. government to
help cover the costs of the war

line of defense
(līn of dĭ-fĕns´)
a line of military force protecting
an area against attack or invasion

minister *(mĭn´ĭ-stər)*
one who conducts religious
services—a clergyman, priest, or
pastor; a *minister* is also a
diplomatic representative sent to
another country.

nations *(nā´shəns)*
countries of the world such as the
U.S., France, Germany, Russia,
etc., each having its own
government

Nobel Peace Prize
(nō-bĕl´ pēs prīz)
international award given to an
individual for promoting peace
between nations or among people
of the same nation

peace court *(pēs kôrt)*
a meeting of people from many
countries to study and pass laws
to keep world peace

political science
(pə-lĭt´ĭ-kəl sī´əns)
a course in school on the
processes, principles, and
structure of government and of
political organizations

politics *(pŏl´ə-tĭks)*
the science of government; the
policies, goals, and activities of a
party within the government

preceptor *(prĭ-sĕp´tər)*
a teacher; under the preceptor
system, students assist professors
and help other students

Progressive party
(prə-grĕs´ĭv pär´tē)
a U.S. political party organized
under the leadership of Theodore
Roosevelt in 1912

quads *(kwŏds)*
buildings built around a
rectangular area to house
students

Quaker school *(kwā´kər skool)*
a school founded by an antiwar
religious group—the Society of
Friends

reason *(rē´zən)*
good judgment; good sense

representatives
(rĕp-rĭ-zĕn´tə-tĭvz)
persons elected or appointed to
serve as authorized agents for
other people or a country; the
members of the lower house of
the U.S. Congress

reverend *(rĕv´ər-ənd)*
title given to a minister or
clergyman of a church

secretary of state
(sĕk´rə-tĕr-ē of stāt)
a member of the U.S. Cabinet,
usually the President's chief
adviser on foreign affairs

social *(sō´shəl)*
a gathering of people for fun

stroke *(strōk)*
a sudden loss of muscular control
and sensation resulting from a
rupture or blocking of a blood
vessel in the brain

tariff *(tăr´ĭf)*
a system of taxes charged by a
government on imported or
exported goods

Texas Ranger
(tĕk´səs rān´jər)
a member of the Texas mounted
police force

torpedoed *(tôr-pē´dōd)*
attacked, damaged, or destroyed
by a self-propelled underwater
explosive device

treaty *(trē´tē)*
a signed, formal agreement
between two or more countries;
contains terms of peace, trade, or
mutual protection

trustees *(trŭs-tēz´)*
persons elected or appointed to
direct the funds and policy of an
institution

Versailles Treaty
(vər-sī´ (Fr.) trē´tē)
treaty signed between the Allies
and Germany after the end of
World War I, stating terms of the
peace settlement

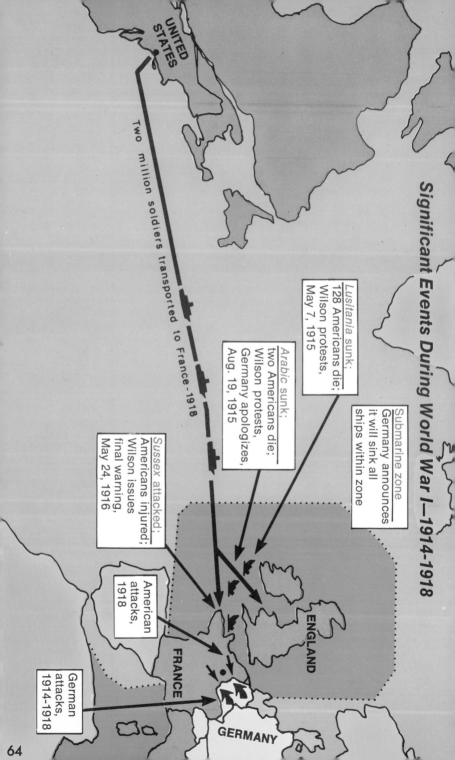

Significant Events During World War I—1914-1918

UNITED STATES

Two million soldiers transported to France-1918

Lusitania sunk;
128 Americans die;
Wilson protests,
May 7, 1915

Arabic sunk:
two Americans die;
Wilson protests,
Germany apologizes,
Aug. 19, 1915

Submarine zone
Germany announces
it will sink all
ships within zone

Sussex attacked:
Americans injured;
Wilson issues
final warning,
May 24, 1916

American
attacks,
1918

ENGLAND

FRANCE

German
attacks,
1914-1918

GERMANY

64